FLUTE

THE BEATLES

Solos and Band Arrangements
Correlated with Essential Elements® Band Method

Arranged by
ROBERT LONGFIELD, JOHNNIE VINSON and JOHN MOSS

Welcome to ESSENTIAL ELEMENTS THE BEATLES! The arrangements in this versatile book can be used either in a full concert band setting or as solos for individual instruments. The SOLO pages appear at the beginning of the book, followed by the BAND ARRANGEMENT pages. The supplemental CD recording or PIANO ACCOMPANIMENT book may be used as an accompaniment for solo performance.

Solo Page	Band Arr. Page	Title	Correlated with Essential Elements
2	13	And I Love Her	Book 1, page 24
3	14	A Hard Day's Night	Book 1, page 34
4	15	Yesterday	Book 1, page 34
5	16	Get Back	Book 1, page 34
6	17	Lady Madonna	Book 2, page 15
7	18	Twist and Shout	Book 2, page 15
8	19	Hey Jude	Book 2, page 15
9	20	Eleanor Rigby	Book 2, page 15
10	21	Ticket to Ride	Book 2, page 32
11	22	Here, There and Everywhere	Book 2, page 32
12	23	I Want to Hold Your Hand	Book 2, page 32

ISBN 978-1-4234-7618-4

7777 W. BLUEMOUND RD. P.O. BOX 13819 MILWAUKEE, WI 53213

Copyright © 2013 by HAL LEONARD CORPORATION
International Copyright Secured   All Rights Reserved

3

From A HARD DAY'S NIGHT

A HARD DAY'S NIGHT

FLUTE
Solo

Words and Music by
JOHN LENNON and PAUL McCARTNEY
Arranged by JOHN MOSS

Copyright © 1964 Sony/ATV Music Publishing LLC
Copyright Renewed
This arrangement Copyright © 2013 Sony/ATV Music Publishing LLC
All Rights Administered by Sony/ATV Music Publishing LLC, 8 Music Square West, Nashville, TN 37203
International Copyright Secured   All Rights Reserved

00860219

Yesterday

FLUTE Solo

Words and Music by
JOHN LENNON and PAUL McCARTNEY
Arranged by JOHN MOSS

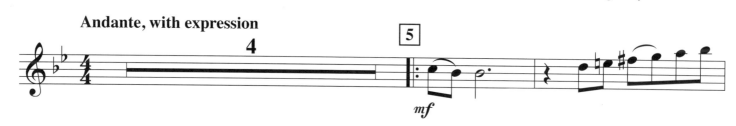

Copyright © 1965 Sony/ATV Music Publishing LLC
Copyright Renewed
This arrangement Copyright © 2013 Sony/ATV Music Publishing LLC
All Rights Administered by Sony/ATV Music Publishing LLC, 8 Music Square West, Nashville, TN 37203
International Copyright Secured   All Rights Reserved

GET BACK

FLUTE Solo

Words and Music by
JOHN LENNON and PAUL McCARTNEY
Arranged by JOHNNIE VINSON

LADY MADONNA

FLUTE Solo

Words and Music by
JOHN LENNON and PAUL McCARTNEY
Arranged by ROBERT LONGFIELD

Copyright © 1968 Sony/ATV Music Publishing LLC
Copyright Renewed
This arrangement Copyright © 2013 Sony/ATV Music Publishing LLC
All Rights Administered by Sony/ATV Music Publishing LLC, 8 Music Square West, Nashville, TN 37203
International Copyright Secured   All Rights Reserved

TWIST AND SHOUT

**Words and Music by
BERT RUSSELL and PHIL MEDLEY**
Arranged by ROBERT LONGFIELD

Copyright © 1964 Sony/ATV Music Publishing LLC and Sloopy II Music
Copyright Renewed
This arrangement Copyright © 2013 Sony/ATV Music Publishing LLC and Sloopy II Music
All Rights on behalf of Sony/ATV Music Publishing LLC Administered by Sony/ATV Music Publishing LLC, 8 Music Square West, Nashville, TN 37203
International Copyright Secured   All Rights Reserved

00860219

HEY JUDE

FLUTE
Solo

Words and Music by
JOHN LENNON and PAUL McCARTNEY
Arranged by ROBERT LONGFIELD

ELEANOR RIGBY

HERE, THERE AND EVERYWHERE

FLUTE Solo

Words and Music by
JOHN LENNON and PAUL McCARTNEY
Arranged by JOHNNIE VINSON

13

From A HARD DAY'S NIGHT
AND I LOVE HER

FLUTE
BAND ARRANGEMENT

Words and Music by
JOHN LENNON and PAUL McCARTNEY
Arranged by JOHNNIE VINSON

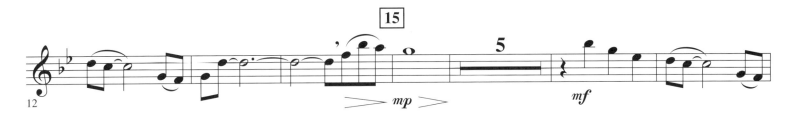

Copyright © 1964 Sony/ATV Music Publishing LLC
Copyright Renewed
This arrangement Copyright © 2013 Sony/ATV Music Publishing LLC
All Rights Administered by Sony/ATV Music Publishing LLC, 8 Music Square West, Nashville, TN 37203
International Copyright Secured   All Rights Reserved

00860219

A HARD DAY'S NIGHT

From A HARD DAY'S NIGHT

Words and Music by JOHN LENNON and PAUL McCARTNEY
Arranged by JOHN MOSS

FLUTE
Band Arrangement

LADY MADONNA

FLUTE
Band Arrangement

Words and Music by
JOHN LENNON and **PAUL McCARTNEY**
Arranged by ROBERT LONGFIELD

Copyright © 1968 Sony/ATV Music Publishing LLC
Copyright Renewed
This arrangement Copyright © 2013 Sony/ATV Music Publishing LLC
All Rights Administered by Sony/ATV Music Publishing LLC, 8 Music Square West, Nashville, TN 37203
International Copyright Secured   All Rights Reserved

HEY JUDE

FLUTE
Band Arrangement

Words and Music by
JOHN LENNON and **PAUL McCARTNEY**
Arranged by ROBERT LONGFIELD

ELEANOR RIGBY

FLUTE
Band Arrangement

Words and Music by
JOHN LENNON and **PAUL McCARTNEY**
Arranged by ROBERT LONGFIELD

Copyright © 1966 Sony/ATV Music Publishing LLC
Copyright Renewed
This arrangement Copyright © 2013 Sony/ATV Music Publishing LLC
All Rights Administered by Sony/ATV Music Publishing LLC, 8 Music Square West, Nashville, TN 37203
International Copyright Secured   All Rights Reserved

I WANT TO HOLD YOUR HAND

FLUTE
Band Arrangement

Words and Music by
JOHN LENNON and **PAUL McCARTNEY**
Arranged by JOHNNIE VINSON

Copyright © 1963 NORTHERN SONGS LTD.
Copyright Renewed
This arrangement Copyright © 2013 NORTHERN SONGS LTD.
All Rights in the United States and Canada Controlled and Administered by SONGS OF UNIVERSAL, INC.
All Rights Reserved   Used by Permission

MORE FAVORITES FROM ESSENTIAL ELEMENTS

These superb collections feature favorite songs that students can play as they progress through their band method books. Each song is arranged to be played by either a full band or by individual soloists, with optional accompaniment on CD.

Each song appears twice in the book, featuring:
- Solo instrument version
- Band arrangement for full band or ensembles
- Pop-style accompaniment CD included with conductor's score
- Accompaniment CD available separately
- Piano accompaniment book that is compatible with recorded backgrounds

Prices:
- Conductor Books $24.99
- Instrument Books $6.99
- Piano Accompaniment Books $11.99
- Accompaniment CDs. $12.99

Instrument books for each collection feature separate books for the following: Flute, Oboe, Bassoon, B♭ Clarinet, E♭ Alto Clarinet, B♭ Bass Clarinet, E♭ Alto Saxophone, B♭ Tenor Saxophone, E♭ Baritone Saxophone, B♭ Trumpet, F Horn, Trombone, Baritone B.C., Baritone T.C., Tuba, Percussion, and Keyboard Percussion.

BROADWAY FAVORITES
Arranged by Michael Sweeney
Songs include:
Beauty and the Beast
Tomorrow
Cabaret
Edelweiss
Don't Cry for Me Argentina
Get Me to the Church on Time
I Dreamed a Dream
Go Go Go Joseph
Memory
The Phantom of the Opera
Seventy Six Trombones

CHRISTMAS FAVORITES
Arranged by Michael Sweeney
Songs include:
The Christmas Song
 (Chestnuts Roasting on an Open Fire)
Frosty the Snow Man
A Holly Jolly Christmas
Jingle-Bell Rock
Let It Snow! Let It Snow! Let It Snow!
Rockin' Around the Christmas Tree
Rudolph, the Red-Nosed Reindeer

FILM FAVORITES
Arranged by Michael Sweeney, John Moss and Paul Lavender
Songs include:
The Black Pearl
Fairytale Opening
Mission: Impossible Theme
My Heart Will Go On
Zorro's Theme
Music from Shrek
May It Be
The Medallion Calls
You'll Be in My Heart
The Rainbow Connection
Accidentally in Love
Also Sprach Zarathustra

MOVIE FAVORITES
Arranged by Michael Sweeney
Includes themes from:
An American Tail
Back to the Future
Chariots of Fire
Apollo 13
E.T.
Forrest Gump
Dances with Wolves
Jurassic Park
The Man from Snowy River
Raiders of the Lost Ark
Star Trek

PATRIOTIC FAVORITES
Arranged by Michael Sweeney
Songs include:
America, the Beautiful
Armed Forces Salute
Battle Hymn of the Republic
God Bless America
Hymn to the Fallen
My Country, 'Tis of Thee (America)
The Patriot
The Star Spangled Banner
Stars and Stripes Forever
This Is My Country
Yankee Doodle/Yankee Dookle Boy

PERFORMANCE FAVORITES, VOL. 1
Arranged by Michael Sweeney, Paul Lavender, John Higgins, John Moss and James Curnow
Songs include:
African Sketches
Barrier Reef
Do You Hear What I Hear
Regimental Honor
Spinning Wheel
You're a Grand Old Flag
British Masters Suite
Elves' Dance
On Broadway
Summon the Heroes
Two Celtic Dances

FOR MORE INFORMATION, SEE YOUR LOCAL MUSIC DEALER, OR WRITE TO:

HAL•LEONARD CORPORATION
7777 W. BLUEMOUND RD. P.O. BOX 13819 MILWAUKEE, WI 53213

Visit Hal Leonard Online at **www.halleonard.com**

Prices, contents, and availability subject to change without notice.
Some products may not be available outside the U.S.A.